First Science Experiments
NIFTY NATURE

by Shar Levine and Leslie Johnstone

illustrations by Steve Harpster

Sterling Publishing Co., Inc.
New York

To Uncle Sam, Aunt Joey, their kids and grandkids; much love.
A special thanks to Cheryl Cohen and Jody Lainoff for their
friendship over the last 4¹/₂ decades.—SL

To my mom, with thanks for getting me off the couch and into the triathlon. I just wish you were a little
slower!—LJ

A special thanks to our wonderful editor, Nancy Sherman, who always makes us look good and sound
even better.

Library of Congress Cataloging-in-Publication Data

Levine, Shar, 1953-
First science experiments : nifty nature / Shar Levine and Leslie Johnstone ; illustrated by Steve
Harpster.
v. cm.
Includes index.
Contents: Plants—Why do leaves change color?—How do plants get water?—Can plants
move?—Wildlife—What do the spots on a ladybug mean?—Why do ants march in a line?—Are
butterflies just pretty moths?—Water—How can you wash water to make it clean?—How do you
get oil out of water?—What happens when you pour things down the drain?—Rocks, dirt,
sand—How do rocks become sand?—What is under my feet?—How can I tell what kind of rock
I've found?—Environment—Can garbage be a good thing?—I'm just a kid! How can I help the
environment?— How can everyone help save natural resources?
ISBN 1-4027-0899-8
1. Science—Experiments—Juvenile literature. 2. Science projects—Juvenile literature. [1.
Science—Experiments. 2. Experiments. 3. Science projects.] I. Johnstone, Leslie. II. Harpster,
Steve, ill. III. Title.
Q164.L4734 2004
507'.8—dc22
2003025631
Edited by Nancy E. Sherman

10 9 8 7 6 5 4 3 2 1
Published by Sterling Publishing Co., Inc.
387 Park Avenue South, New York, NY 10016
© 2004 by Shar Levine and Leslie Johnstone
Distributed in Canada by Sterling Publishing
^{c}/o Canadian Manda Group, One Atlantic Avenue,
Suite 105 Toronto, Ontario, Canada M6K 3E7
Distributed in Great Britain and Europe
by Chris Lloyd at Orca Book Services,
Stanley House, Fleets Lane, Poole BH15 3AJ, England
Distributed in Australia by Capricorn Link (Australia) Pty. Ltd.
P.O. Box 704, Windsor, NSW 2756, Australia

Printed in China
All rights reserved

Sterling ISBN 1-4027-0899-8

Contents

Note to Parents and Teachers

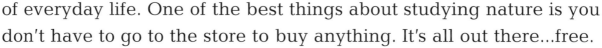

This book is designed to answer very basic questions young children have about nature. Kids are curious about the world around them, and looking at nature is a simple way to start discovering the science of everyday life. One of the best things about studying nature is you don't have to go to the store to buy anything. It's all out there...free.

Obviously we can't explain all the mysteries of nature, but we can start you and your child on the road to discovery. Along the way you may be surprised to learn something new, too. If your child wants to know more about a specific topic, you can visit the library to find a book on the subject. Surf the Internet with your child and research the question using a search engine where you can type in your question and be directed to a number of sites that may provide answers. Make a list or diary of your child's questions and work with your child to find the answers. Just think of the things you may discover together!

Safety First: These activities are designed to be as safe and simple as possible. Some adult supervision is suggested with small children, especially when performing experiments outdoors. Please read the **Be Safe** checklist with your child before starting any of the activities.

Be Safe

DO

✔ Before starting, ask an adult for permission to do the experiment.

✔ Read through each experiment with an adult first.

✔ If you have allergies or asthma, let a parent decide which experiments you can safely do.

✔ Have an adult handle anything that is sharp or made of glass.

✔ Keep babies and pets away from experiments and supplies.

✔ Wash your hands when you are finished.

✔ Keep your work area clean. Wipe up spills right away.

✔ Tell an adult right away if you or anyone else gets hurt!

DON'T

✔ Don't put any part of these experiments in your mouth.

✔ Never look directly at the sun or go out without a hat, sunscreen, and insect repellant.

✔ Never touch or harm spiders, stinging insects, or snakes.

✔ Never go out during a thunderstorm or dangerous windstorm.

Introduction

Look out a window and what do you see? No matter where you are, you can see some part of nature. The beauty of the natural world is all around you, from the clouds in the sky to the dirt on the ground, and everywhere in between. See that tiny ant scurrying across the porch? Don't crush it! Take a moment instead to watch where it's going and what it's doing.

Do you think of science as rocket ships and test tubes, chemicals and computers? Well, there's science in nature, too. Have you ever wondered why leaves change color in the fall or ants march in a line?

This book may help explain some of life's little mysteries. It will help you begin to see that there's more to science than meets the eye.

Plants, for instance, are really important to every living thing. Close your eyes and imagine the world without plants. Instead of a place rich with life and color, earth would be a sandy desert. All living things would die because they would have nothing to eat. Even rivers and lakes would die. In the first section, you will begin to see how wonderful plants really are.

Did You Know?

When you buy bananas in the grocery store, you generally choose unripe or green ones. After a few days on the counter, the bananas turn a deep yellow, much as leaves do in the fall in some places, and for the same reason (see page 10). Then they're ready to eat.

Plants

To begin to see the wonder of plants, let's first take a look at seeds. The variety of their shapes and sizes alone is amazing. Plants spread their seeds in many ways. Some, like maple trees, have seeds with special shapes that let them hitch a ride on a breeze to their new home. Other seeds have sharp bristles that attach to animal fur and get carried to new places. Still others, like those of apples and pears, get eaten with their fruit by passing animals. The seeds pass right through the animals and become part of a rich fertilizer.

Fruit trees like papaya have yet another way to spread their seeds: the fruit stays on the tree, but the bottom gets really soft and the seeds just drop out of the rotting fruit.

In some ways, it would be nice if fruit didn't have seeds. In fact, for many years, there have been seedless oranges and grapes in the grocery store...even seedless watermelons. But if these fruit don't have seeds, how do they start new plants? Scientists have ways of creating fruit that nature never dreamed of. With seedless fruit, shoots or buds from the original plant are rooted or **grafted** onto similar growing plants, where they grow and mature (see bolded words in Glossary, page 47).

Look at the fruits and vegetables you eat. Can you see the seeds?

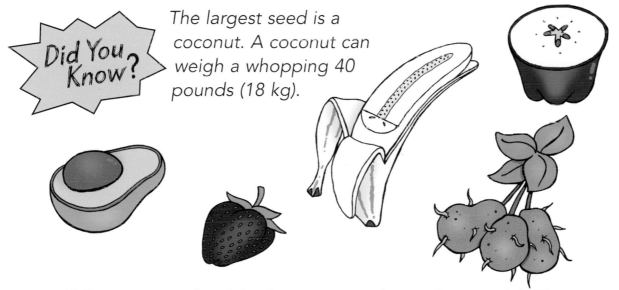

Did You Know?

The largest seed is a coconut. A coconut can weigh a whopping 40 pounds (18 kg).

When you work with plants, remember to be careful. If you want just a leaf or a flower, don't pull the whole plant up by the roots. Have an adult help you cut or pick what you need. Don't raid a park or your neighbor's garden. Ask for permission first. And if you're not sure if a plant is safe to touch, ask an adult.

Why do leaves change color

Where the weather is always warm, the trees may be green all year round. But where the summers are warm and the weather cools suddenly in the autumn, the leaves often turn brilliant shades of red, orange, and yellow. Exactly why does this happen?

You need

- coffee filter
- scissors
- leaf from a tree or plant
- spoon
- tape
- rubbing alcohol
- lidded glass jar, 6 inches (15 cm) tall

Do this

1 From the coffee filter, cut a strip 6 inches (15 cm) x 1 inch (2.5 cm). Place the leaf—either side up—on top of the coffee filter strip, 1 inch (2.5 cm) from the end.

2 Rub the leaf with the spoon handle to make a green line or streak across the narrow side of the strip.

3 Tape the end of the strip farther from the streak to the inside of the jar lid.

4 Have an adult pour $1/4$ cup (40 mL) of rubbing alcohol into the jar to cover the bottom. Lower the strip into the alcohol and close the lid on the jar. Watch the strip for several minutes. What do you see?

5 Have an adult take the strip out of the jar and let it dry.

What happened?

As the alcohol moved up the filter strip, it passed through the green streak of pigment and took it along for the ride. This green pigment is chlorophyll. Made up of tiny particles called **molecules**, it makes leaves green and helps them use sunlight to grow. Bigger molecules travel more slowly than smaller ones. Eventually they separate on the strip, so you see different bands of color.

The truth is that leaves don't really change color; they just lose chlorophyll. When it gets very cold in the fall, the leaves die and their chlorophyll breaks down. Then we see other pigments left behind in the leaves.

How do plants get water

When you're thirsty, you can go to the fridge for a juice box or just get some water from the tap. But plants don't have things like electricity, plumbing, and appliances. So what do they do?

You need

- ♣ leaf
- ♣ water
- ♣ small plastic bottle
- ♣ modeling clay
- ♣ drinking straws
- ♣ friend or mirror
- ♣ magnifying glass (optional)

Do this

1 Pluck a leaf from a tree or plant, leaving a long stem.

2 Fill a small bottle (like that used for bottled water) to 1 inch (2.5 cm) from the top with tap water.

3 Wrap a flattened piece of modeling clay around the top of the bottle. Poke the stem of the plant through the clay, making sure it touches the water.

4 Push the straw through a small hole in the clay; stop it above the water. Be sure not to get clay in the straw. Seal the clay around the straw and the leaf stem.

5 Have a friend watch the leaf as you use the straw to suck out the air in the bottle. Then put in a new straw and watch what happens as your friend sucks out the air through the straw.

6 Try this with different kinds of leaves. Does the size of the leaf make a difference?

What happened?

Leaves are specially designed to help plants breathe and drink. They take in air and water in much the same way you used the straw. If you look at the underside of a leaf with a magnifying glass, you may see tiny holes, or **stomata**. These are the openings to long tubes inside the plant stem. When you sucked the air out of the sealed bottle, the leaf replaced it by drawing air in from the outside. You can see this in the bubbles released out the cut end of the stem. Just like you, plants can't live without air.

Can plants move

If you have a cat or a dog, you may have seen it curl up to sleep in a warm, sunny spot. As the sun moves, your pet may move too, so it can keep basking in the rays. But did you know that plants enjoy sunlight just as much as animals do?

You need

❖ potted flowering plant
❖ sunny window

Do this

1 In the morning, turn the pot so that the plant's flowers or leaves are facing the inside of the room, away from the light.

2 Throughout the day, check which way the flowers and leaves are facing. Do they follow the movement of the sun?

3 If it is summer, watch the flower heads in the garden. Do they move, too?

What happened?

The leaves and flowers turned to follow the sun. The sun's stronger light on one side of the stem activated chemicals in the plant that made one side grow faster than the other. This made the stem bend, tilting the leaves and flowers toward the sun. The word for this growth response to sunlight is phototropism, *photo* referring to light, and *tropism* referring to turning or curving.

Did You Know?

Here's another new word for you: nyctitropism. How does this relate to what you just learned? You found that in daylight, plants move to follow the sun. Well, at night, just like you, the leaves and flower petals of the plant come to rest in a neutral position. The word to describe this is— you guessed it—nyctitropism.

Wildlife

When you think of wildlife, big furry things like bears or lions may come to mind. But where would the average kid find wild creatures? A visit to a park, a forest, even your own backyard may bring a close encounter with beasts of many kinds.

In this section, you will start to see the value of even the smallest of living things. The most important thing is that they remain alive and unharmed after your meeting. Don't bother the bugs, worms, or birds you observe. Be very careful— getting too up close and personal with even little wild things has its hazards. Be sure to keep a safe distance from wasps, bees, and other stinging insects. Even tiny ants can band together and bite you.

You may find that some animals are awfully hard to see. To fool your eyes and keep you

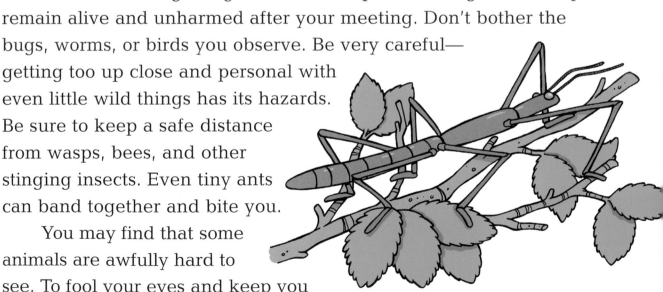

away, and to keep certain birds and other insects from seeing them at all, these animals use **camouflage**. Their shape and color help them hide. Some may look like leaves or twigs on the plants where they live. There are insects that are mimics: they look like other insects that taste bad to birds, so the birds leave them alone. Still other animals blend into their surroundings, as a white coat blends into a snowy background. And a green **algae** that grows in certain sloths' hair makes them the same color as the trees they live in.

Did You Know?

There's an insect in England that you might say has changed its spots over time. The Peppered Moth comes in two colors, light gray and dark gray. The light gray ones were much more common than the dark ones in the 1800s: the dark variety was easy for birds to see against the light-colored tree trunks, and they were eaten. As industrial development polluted the air and darkened the tree bark, the lighter moths' camouflage became ineffective, so they were more easily seen and eaten by birds. This meant that more dark moths survived. However, over the years, the air became cleaner and the color advantage shifted again. Once again, there are fewer dark gray moths.

Why do ladybugs have spots

If you don't really like the thought of a beetle on your body, you're not alone. But how about a ladybug? That's not so bad. Ladybugs are nice and harmless. They'll just walk on your body until it's time to fly away home. Let's take a closer look at ladybugs. **NOTE**: Be very gentle with this delicate bug. Do not pick it up between your fingers, hold its wings, or squish it.

You need
- ❖ladybug
- ❖magnifying glass

Do this

1 Find a ladybug on a tree, leaf, or vegetable. Hold your finger out for the bug to walk onto or use a leaf to scoop it up.

2 Take a closer look at your new friend with a magnifying glass. Can you find its head? Its mouth? How many legs does the ladybug have? Do you see the tips of the ladybug's wings sticking out under its spotted wing cases?

3 Place the bug on your palm and slowly turn your palm down. The bug will walk to the edge. Can you feel its tiny feet?

4 With the ladybug on a flat surface, flip it onto its back with your fingertip. Don't worry—this isn't harmful, like flipping a turtle. Watch how the bug turns itself over.

What happened?

Ladybugs are a kind of beetle and there are over 4,000 different kinds of them—about 400 in the United States alone. And ladybugs don't all look alike. Some have red wing covers, some, orange or yellow, with any number of dots, or even stripes!

Those marks are a ladybug's shield against hungry birds. You can't tell, but ladybugs smell terrible and taste even worse. A bird will eat a ladybug only once and avoid bugs with similar markings forever after.

Ladybugs are a farmer's friend: they eat other insects that destroy crops, so no pesticides are needed when they're around. And ladybugs love to eat—each one can devour over 100 aphids a day!

Why do ants march in a line?

You may know the song that starts, "The ants go marching one by one, hurrah, hurrah...." Your parents may even have sung it when they were kids. This raises the question: why do ants go marching in a line? Let's find out. **NOTE**: Don't get too close to an ants' nest. If the colony feels threatened, it may try to attack YOU!

You need

- ✤ ants
- ✤ sugar
- ✤ fruit or small piece of candy
- ✤ book
- ✤ old CD

Do this

1 Watch your sidewalk or garden for a line of ants. If you can't find one, place a little sugar on the sidewalk. Ants will quickly find the food.

2 Watch the ants. Are they carrying any food?

3 Place an object such as a book or a CD in the ants' path, being careful not to squish any of the ants. What happens when they discover their path is blocked?

4 Once the ants are settled into their new path, replace the object with another one. What do the ants do this time?

5 Remove the object. Gently blow on an ant so it goes off the path. What does the ant do now?

6 Place a small piece of candy or fruit on the sidewalk. Watch how the ants get the food back to their nest.

What happened?

Ants are pretty smart for their size. They always seek the shortest route from their food to the nest. You saw that even when an obstacle is put in their path, ants find their way again. You can't see it or smell it, but ants leave a trail of chemicals called **pheromones** that guides other ants. Each ant follows the scent of the ants that went before it. When something gets in the ant's way, it finds a new way. Soon, all the insects find the newer, shorter path and stop using the old long one.

Are butterflies just pretty moths?

Butterflies are beautiful. Their delicate wings bear rich designs in colors ranging from deep metallic blue to palest yellow. If you'd like to know more about them, simply watching is a great way to learn.

You need

- adult helper
- your own yard or neighborhood, a public park or gardening space, or an indoor butterfly garden

Do this

1 Have an adult go with you to one of the places mentioned above and spend some time among the flowering plants. Try to find a local museum or garden that is holding an exhibit featuring butterflies flying free within a controlled environment.

2 Watch the plants for signs of butterflies and moths. Do not disturb them.

3 Draw pictures of some of the butterflies and moths you see.

What happened?

You got a good look at both moths and butterflies. Here's a foolproof way to tell the difference between them: when the insect lands, take a close look at its wings. If they are folded up and held together above the insect's body, it's a butterfly. A moth's wings fold down and over its body. In addition, the antennae of a butterfly resemble upside down baseball bats, while the moth's antennae look like feathers.

These insects have four stages of life, in some of which you might not even recognize them. They start as eggs and grow into **caterpillars**, little wiggly wormlike forms. Then they create **cocoons**, small hard shells in which to wait until they become butterflies and moths. Did you see any cocoons?

Did You Know?

The largest butterfly is found in Papua, New Guinea. The Queen Alexandra's Birdwing has a wingspan that can exceed 11 inches (28 cm)!

Water

If you were to see Earth from space—or just look at a globe—you'd see that most of the planet is covered by water. And this water doesn't just stay put. It goes through a cycle. No, not like a bike, silly.

A cycle describes the recurring changes that water is continually undergoing. In a process called **evaporation**, it is changed by the sun's heat from water in the ocean to a gas or **vapor**. Heat carries the water vapor up into the sky, where it changes again by the process of **condensation**: it cools and joins other water molecules to form clouds. You've seen that dark, stormy clouds drop rain and snow. The drops and flakes fall from the sky, showering trees and towns, people and wildlife. The water that is not absorbed runs off into rivers, lakes, and oceans, and, yes...the whole thing starts again.

"The Rime of the Ancient Mariner" is a poem about a sailor who is stranded at sea and dying of thirst. "Water, water everywhere, Nor any drop to drink," he cries. If you have ever been in the ocean, you surely know that the water is very salty. The more you drink, the thirstier you become. How did the oceans get to be so salty anyway?

When water falls from the sky as rain or snow, some of it runs off into streams and rivers. As it flows, the water picks up mineral salts in the ground. The water finds its way back to the ocean, where a good portion of it evaporates, leaving behind the salt. Your body has no way to get rid of the extra salt in seawater. In fact, if you try to drink it, it will just make you more thirsty.

Scientists have developed ways to extract the salt from seawater, using the natural processes of evaporation and condensation, so that people can drink it. But some seabirds have organs above their eyes that remove the salt from  seawater, enabling the birds to drink salty water. The albatross, the bird featured in "The Rime of the Ancient Mariner," didn't have the sailor's problem. This bird can drink seawater because it has its own salt remover right on its face.

How can you make water cleaner ❓

If your hands are dirty, you can use soap and water to clean up before you dig into dinner. But what happens when your water is dirty? You can't use soap and water to make water clean. In many places, there isn't enough clean or unpolluted water for people to drink. So what do they do?

You need

- water
- grass
- sand
- coffee filter
- pebbles
- plastic jars
- adult helper
- dirt
- leaves
- large plastic soda pop bottle
- crushed piece of charcoal (without lighter fluid)

Do this

1 Mix dirt, grass, leaves, and pebbles in a jar and add lots of water. Swirl the mixture around in the jar. There should be enough water for the mess to swirl freely.

2 Have an adult cut the top ¹/₄ off a plastic pop bottle. This top is the holder for your coffee filter.

3 Place the filter in the holder, then drop the holder into a second jar, with the holder's mouth pointing downward.

4 Gently layer the charcoal, sand, pebbles, dirt—even leaves from your garden—into the filter.

5 Pour the dirty water into the filter and watch the color as it flows into the jar. DO NOT DRINK THIS WATER!

What happened?

Your filter took out a lot of the gucky stuff. But the water is still not good to drink because tiny things like bacteria and viruses can get through the filter. Some places have very dirty water and people who drink it get very sick. The further away the water's source, the more likely it is to be polluted. If water comes from a river that is polluted upstream, it may carry fertilizer, chemicals, and waste from sewers and animals. People around the world are working to make water cleaner and safer for drinking.

How do oil spills hurt sea life?

Oil doesn't mix with water, but sometimes it gets released into the ocean. Then what happens?

You need

- ✤2 bowls
- ✤water
- ✤feathers
- ✤towel
- ✤vegetable oil
- ✤dishwashing liquid

Do this

1. Fill a small bowl with cool water. Quickly dip a feather in the water. Shake the feather. Does the water stick to the feather? Pat the feather dry with the towel.

2. Add a tablespoon of oil to the water. Dip the feather into the bowl to coat it with oil. Hold the feather up. Does it keep its shape? Pat the feather with a towel. Does the feather look as it did in step 1?

3. Fill a second bowl with water and dip the oily feather into it. Does the water clean the feather?

4 Gently mix a bit of dishwashing liquid into the water in the second bowl. Dip the oily feather into the bowl and rub it gently in the soapy water. Does the oil come off?

5 Mix the oil and water in the bowl. Can you think of a way to take out the oil?

What happened?

Feathers resist water. They keep birds warm and help them float. But when feathers get coated with oil, they absorb water; they get wet and heavy. Birds can die. Detergent can remove the oil and return the feathers to their natural condition.

Oil spills are a threat to birds and to all wildlife. Oil tankers, giant ships that carry oil, sometimes leak. The leaking oil pollutes the water. But even more oil pollution comes from the changed engine oil in cars. Used car oil should be recycled. It shouldn't go in the garbage or down the drain.

There are volunteer groups that rescue sea birds and animals caught in oil spills. Volunteers wash the animals to remove the oil, and care for them until they can be safely released.

What happens to things you put down the drain ❓

The next time you pull the plug in your bathtub, watch as the water swirls down the drain. Where does it go and what happens when it gets there? Do you think the fish in the ocean will enjoy your favorite body scrub? Let's see.

You need

- ✤ large glass bowl, like a fish bowl—but please, no fish!
- ✤ liquid plant fertilizer or powdered fish food

Do this

1 This is not a fish-friendly activity, so please use an old fish bowl without the creatures. Wash the bowl and have an adult help you fill it with water.

2 With an adult to help, place the bowl on a flat surface in a bright, sunny spot near a window.

3 Sprinkle several tablespoons of fish food or plant fertilizer on the water. Let the bowl sit undisturbed for a week. What color is the water?

4 Add another tablespoon of fish or plant food to the bowl. Wait another week. What do you see now?

What happened

It may not be the scum of the universe, but you'll see a lot of gross green gunk in your bowl. This gunk is algae, a simple fast-growing plant-like life form that lives in water on nutrients from soap and waste. An excess of algae uses up the oxygen in the water and leaves fish without enough oxygen to live. Fish-eating animals and birds no longer have food. Other wildlife must move away, or die.

Just as water runs from rivers and streams into the oceans, the water from your drains at home and from the streets and sidewalks of your town flows into the ocean. And the water carries with it all the things that everyone has put there. As all these nasty things build up, they can cause fish to sicken and die. So be careful what you put down the drain. Don't use products that can harm the environment. Be sure the labels on your bubble bath and shampoo say they are biodegradable. Biodegradable means they will break down over time into chemicals that are safe for living things.

Rocks, Dirt, Sand

What's the oldest thing around your house? No, it's not your grandparents. There's something probably far older just beyond your front door. Go outside and look down. Do you see any dust? Dust is a rock that has really broken down. No matter where you go, you can find some kind of rock—even on the deepest sea floor. What about volcanos? Well, red-hot flowing lava is simply melted rock.

Pick up a rock and take a good look at it. Is it smooth or pointy? Squeeze it. Is it hard or soft? Drop it on the ground. Does it crack or break? Is it one color or many? Does it sparkle? All these things tell a story. No, not a bedtime story. They tell how rocks are formed.

We classify or sort rocks by how they are formed. Igneous rocks come from volcanos. Sedimentary rocks are compressed layers of sand deposited by water. Metamorphic rocks are one form of rock changed by heat or pressure into another. Wherever you live, you don't have to go far to find a rock. Concrete and cement are made from crushed rocks and glass is melted sand.

If you've ever built sand castles on the beach, you've seen that sand has tiny bits of rock and ground-up shells. Sand that's soft to walk on usually doesn't have many shells. Sharp sand that hurts your bare feet may have broken shells or coral in it. Black sand beaches, like those in Hawaii, have broken bits of lava from volcanos. The waves pounding on the shore break down the rocks and shells into tiny grains of sand.

If you look closely at sand, you'll see lots of black grains. Scientists have recently discovered that these grains, a magnetic material called magnetite, come from bacteria deep under the ocean. Just as we breathe oxygen, these microscopic life forms breathe iron. In the process of breathing, they produce magnetite.

In this section, you will learn a great deal more about the rocks in your everyday life. So get ready to rock on.

How do rocks become sand?

Unlike ice, which is frozen water, rocks don't melt. But they do break down to become sand and, believe it or not, water is a part of that process. How can this be? Let's find out.

You need

❖sand from the beach
❖sand shovel
❖adult helper
NOTE: MAKE SURE YOU WEAR SUN BLOCK AND THAT AN ADULT IS NEARBY WHEN YOU ARE CLOSE TO OR IN THE WATER. THE WAVES CAN BE DANGEROUS.

Do this

1 The next time you are at the beach, spend some time sifting through sand from different areas. Choose an area far away from the water, one 5 feet (2 m) from the water's edge, and one 3 feet (1 m) into the water.

2 Look for flat objects that appear frosted or clouded, perhaps in colors like blue, green, or brown.

What happened?

You found that sand is a lot more than just tiny sharp grains. Among other things, you probably saw many colored objects in the sand with frosty, etched surfaces. These are most likely bits of broken glass that have been worn and rounded by the tides. When water runs over hard materials like rocks and glass in rivers and streams, it breaks off tiny bits and erodes—or wears away—the material's surface, leaving it smoother. These tiny broken bits of rock and glass become part of the sand you see at the shore.

Temperature changes cause rocks to crack and break too, just as you may have seen pavement do on city streets.

What is under my feet?

If you really want to get the dirt on soil, just go out and take a good hard look at it. It will open up a whole new world to you.

You need

❖small metal garden shovel
❖soft ground
❖adult helper

Do this

1 Take a walk with an adult. If you're near a forest, river, or park, look for an area where the soil is exposed, like the side of a bank or a cliff. Can you see the different colors of earth? If you're in the city, look for a construction pit for a new building. The different soil layers are easy to see from the safety of the street.

2 Ask an adult to help you find a safe spot where you can dig a small hole. Use a shovel to dig just under the top layer of soil. What do you find?

3 Dig a little deeper, until the soil starts changing colors. What do you see now?

4 Now dig another layer. How deep did you have to go this time before the dirt changed colors?

What happened?

It may have surprised you to see that dirt comes in different colors. Just under the grass and twigs, the first layer was probably dark brown or black. This is the topsoil, a layer rich in nutrients deposited by earthworms and essential to plant life. The next layer may be a lighter brown color because of leaching, the removal of salts and minerals by water that has flowed through it. Below this may have been a reddish-brown layer, perhaps with tiny pebbles and gravel or larger rocks and stones. This is the subsoil. You probably didn't reach bedrock, the underlying rock layer.

Geologists are scientists who study rocks and soil. They can tell the age of the different layers of soil and rock and what the climate was like at the time each of them was formed.

How can I tell one rock from another

It can be very hard to tell one rock from another just by looking. But rocks are made of minerals, and you can tell minerals apart by their different properties. One mineral, pyrite, looks so much like gold, it's actually called "fool's gold." You can probably find good rock samples right in your own backyard. But how do you tell them apart? Here's a way to rate your rocks.

You need

- rocks
- paper
- soap
- sandpaper
- resealable plastic bags
- pencil
- iron nail
- old dull butter knife
- water
- penny

Do this

1 Take a walk with an adult and gather a number of rocks in plastic bags. Keep a record of where you find each one.

2 When you get home, rinse the rocks off in soapy water and let them dry. Put each rock back in the bag you used to collect it.

3 Take a sample rock and use it to try to scratch the iron nail, the penny, the sandpaper, and an old dull butter knife.

4 Try this test with each of the rocks you collected. Which rocks were able to scratch the most items? Which the least? Lay your rocks in order, from the fewest scratches made to the most.

What happened?

Some rocks were able to scratch every material, while others could scratch only one or two. Mineralogists, scientists who study rocks, determine the hardness of different rocks using similar techniques, as this is an important clue to a rock's identity.

A rock's color and surface texture (whether glassy or rough) also help identify it. Other identifying clues lie in whether the rock has crystals or grains, and whether it's solid or spongy or layered.

The hardest rock of all is a diamond. Only another diamond can scratch a diamond.

Environment

Now that you know a little more about the natural world, you understand how important it is to living things everywhere that you protect it. You can be a partner in saving the earth by practicing what are called the 3 R's: reduce, reuse, recycle. These simple good acts can help preserve the environment.

Reduce the amount of garbage you make. One way to do this is to buy items with less packaging. Another is not to buy things you don't need. You can make some things yourself, like greeting cards, wrapping paper, and picture frames, from stuff you already have at home. Read labels and buy things that are biodegradable.

Reuse items you have already. Take plastic or cloth bags with you when you buy groceries. Wash out plastic or glass containers and use them to store things.

Recycle paper, plastic, glass, and metal. If you have a recycling program in your area, use it. If you don't have one, write to your elected officials to see if you can start one. Try to buy recycled products, such as paper and plastics.

You know that lunch you take to school every day? It makes a lot more trash than you may realize. If you put those wrappers, juice boxes, and sandwich bags together with all your other trash for a year, did you know it might amount to as much as 1,000 pounds (450 kg)? That's what the average person throws out in a year. Simply taking a lunch with reusable plastic containers can reduce garbage, literally by tons.

Did You Know?

If you've ever been to a garbage dump or landfill, you've seen how huge an area it can cover. It can easily be 20 feet (6 m) deep and cover tens of acres. So what happens to all that stuff? Often, it just sits there. It may stay the same size, shape, and weight for 30 or 40 years, or even longer! Some landfills are eventually put to other uses; the mountains of garbage become parks or recreational areas. But think how much better it would be never to make the garbage in the first place.

How can I reduce garbage?

What else can you do to help the environment? Did you ever think about saving up your garbage and using it? Probably not. It may sound pretty gross, but it's a good way to help the earth.

You need

- vegetable kitchen waste
- large pail with a lid
- shovel
- leaves or cut grass
- adult helper

Do this

1 Save your vegetable garbage, like banana peels, potato skins, and rotting tomatoes, in a pail. Do not save meat, bones, fat, cheese, milk, or anything else from animals. Do not save plastics, glass, or paper. Do not put kitty litter in the pail.

2 Have an adult help you choose an appropriate place to age the vegetable material in your yard or in a public gardening space. Make it a shady, sheltered area of dirt.

3 When the pail is about half full, take it out to your selected **compost** area. Spread out a shallow layer of the garbage.

4 Scatter leaves or grass over the garbage. Add another layer of garbage over this each time your pail is half full. Always top the pile with leaves or grass.

5 Sprinkle the compost lightly with water every few days. Don't soak the pile, just dampen it.

6 When the pile is about 3 feet (1 m) high, ask an adult helper to turn it with a shovel.

What happened?

Your saved-up garbage decayed, becoming food for bacteria and earthworms. These little creatures helped produce a nutrient-rich all-natural organic fertilizer for your garden. Spread this rich, dark fertilizer around your trees and flowers. It will feed them, protect their roots from heat and frost, and keep them from drying out, so you'll be able to use less water.

I'm just a kid!
How can I help the environment

How would it be to live without running water, electricity, heat, or air conditioning? Energy is needed for all these things and it comes from many sources: wind, water, the sun, and the burning of fuels. But we risk running out of some of these resources, and using some of them can pollute our air and water. So the less energy we use, the better— for now and for the future, for all of us. Here's one way to help.

You need

❖bathtub   ❖ruler   ❖water   ❖adult helper

Do this

1 Have an adult run a bath for you. NEVER PLAY IN THE TUB WITHOUT AN ADULT AROUND. Use a ruler to measure the depth of the bath water in the tub. How deep is it?

2 Next, drain the water and have an adult run a shower for you. Plug the drain so you can see how much water you used in your shower. How deep is the water after your shower?

What happened?

You might have expected otherwise, but you found that the shower used less water than the bath, meaning you saved both water and the energy to heat it.

You learned earlier that water has a cycle. One interesting effect of water's continual recycling is that there is as much water in the world today as there was millions of years ago. In fact, it's the same water. Molecules that dinosaurs drank could be in the very water from your faucet!

Did You Know?

How can everyone help save natural resources?

Here are some more simple ways you can save energy and water around your home.

1 Don't run tap water to get it cold. Instead, keep a jug of water in the fridge. It will always be cold and ready to drink. Add a slice of lemon for flavor.

2 Prevent drips and save water by turning off all the taps.

3 Wet your toothbrush, then turn off the water. You don't need to run water while brushing your teeth.

4 Use a bucket of water instead of a hose to help your parents wash their cars or to wash your bike.

5 Turn off lights, TVs, and radios when you aren't using them.

6 For short trips to school or the store, walk or ride your bike instead of taking the car.

7 Turn down the heat a couple of degrees in the winter and wear socks and a sweater if you're cold. In the summer, wear lighter clothes to keep cool and save on air conditioning.

Glossary

algae-simple, green, plantlike life forms that generally live in water

camouflage-coloring or markings used to blend into surroundings

caterpillar-wormlike early stage in the life of a moth or butterfly

cocoon-a hard shell or casing in which a moth or butterfly waits to mature

compost-decaying plant material used as fertilizer

condensation-the change from a gas to a liquid, or the liquid itself

evaporation-the change from a liquid to a gas or vapor

grafting-attaching a bud or shoot from one plant to a similar growing plant on which the bud or shoot can grow into a mature plant

molecule-the smallest particles that make up compounds like water or sugar

pheromones-chemicals given off by an animal as a signal to others of its kind

stomata-pores in leaves through which gases enter a plant

vapor-the gas form of a thing that can also be a solid or a liquid

Index